Friction

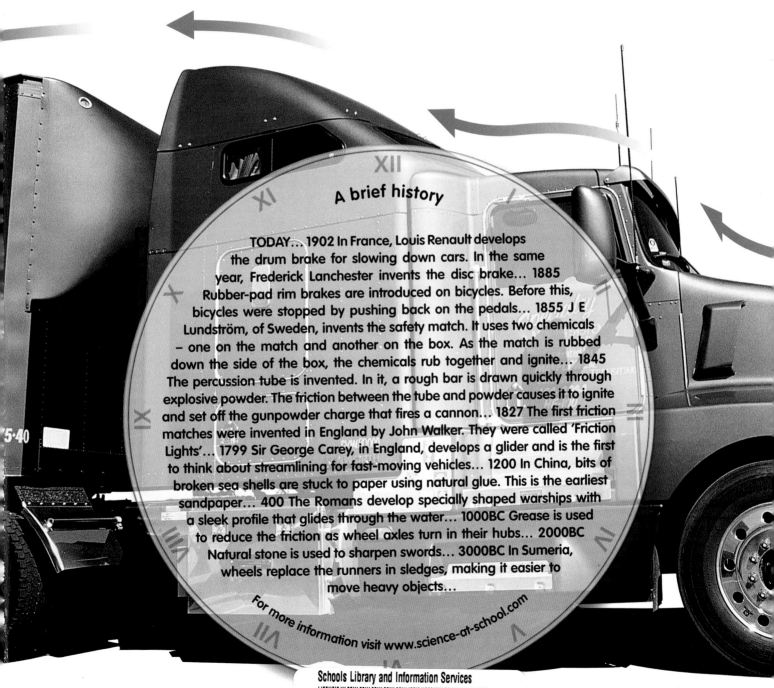

A brief history

TODAY... 1902 In France, Louis Renault develops the drum brake for slowing down cars. In the same year, Frederick Lanchester invents the disc brake... 1885 Rubber-pad rim brakes are introduced on bicycles. Before this, bicycles were stopped by pushing back on the pedals... 1855 J E Lundström, of Sweden, invents the safety match. It uses two chemicals – one on the match and another on the box. As the match is rubbed down the side of the box, the chemicals rub together and ignite... 1845 The percussion tube is invented. In it, a rough bar is drawn quickly through explosive powder. The friction between the tube and powder causes it to ignite and set off the gunpowder charge that fires a cannon... 1827 The first friction matches were invented in England by John Walker. They were called 'Friction Lights'... 1799 Sir George Carey, in England, develops a glider and is the first to think about streamlining for fast-moving vehicles... 1200 In China, bits of broken sea shells are stuck to paper using natural glue. This is the earliest sandpaper... 400 The Romans develop specially shaped warships with a sleek profile that glides through the water... 1000BC Grease is used to reduce the friction as wheel axles turn in their hubs... 2000BC Natural stone is used to sharpen swords... 3000BC In Sumeria, wheels replace the runners in sledges, making it easier to move heavy objects...

For more information visit www.science-at-school.com

Word list

These are some science words that you should look out for as you go through the book. They are shown using CAPITAL letters.

AIR RESISTANCE
The amount that air pushes back when something moves through it. Air resistance is greatest when a large object is moving quickly.

AQUAPLANING
Uncontrolled gliding of car or bike tyres when they travel fast over a wet road.

AVALANCHE
A very rapid movement of snow down a mountainside. An avalanche often occurs when thick snow is disturbed. Skiers often cause avalanches, but sometimes even a clap of thunder, or even a handclap, is enough to shake some snow free and begin the avalanche.

EVAPORATE
When a liquid turns into a gas.

FLEXIBLE
Something which bends easily to a new shape.

FORCE
A push or a pull. A force has a size and also works in a direction.

FORCEMETER
An instrument for measuring the size of a force. It is usually made of a spring.

FRICTION
A force that works against any movement.

GRIP
A stickiness that makes things hold fast.

LUBRICANT
A liquid that is used to make two surfaces glide more easily past one another.

NEWTON
The measurement used for force. A weight of 1kg is equal to a force of ten newtons.

SLIDE
When one surface slips very easily over another one.

STREAMLINING
Making something a sleek shape so that it will move through air or water as easily as possible.

TREAD
The pattern on an object such as the sole of a shoe or the surface of a tyre. It is designed to give a good grip on both dry and wet surfaces.

WATER RESISTANCE
The amount that water pushes back against something moving through it. Water resistance is greatest when a flat surface tries to push through the water quickly. Water resistance is very much greater than air resistance.

WEIGHT
The force with which an object is attracted to the Earth by gravity.

Contents

Weblink: www.CurriculumVisions.com

What is friction?

Friction is a natural grip, or stickiness, that stops things slipping uncontrollably past one another.

We have all slipped on a floor (Picture 1) or tried to pull open a drawer that simply doesn't want to move. Things are either more slippery or more sticky than we expect. In everything we do, we experience a hidden natural 'stickiness' or 'GRIP' between things that touch. It is called FRICTION.

What causes friction?

If you were to be able to look very, very closely at the place where two objects touch, you would see that the surfaces are made of tiny bumps and troughs (Picture 2).

▼▶ (Picture 1) You slip on a banana skin because the friction of the banana skin is less than that of your shoes, so the foot on the banana skin moves forward faster than you expect. This causes you to lose your balance.

NOTE In this book a magnifying glass is used to show a very close-up view. In most cases you would need a far higher magnification than a magnifying glass to see what is shown in the picture.

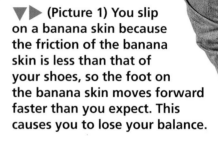

◀ (Picture 2) When you look at surfaces very closely, you find they have bumps and troughs that interlock. This is what keeps most surfaces from gliding over each other easily.

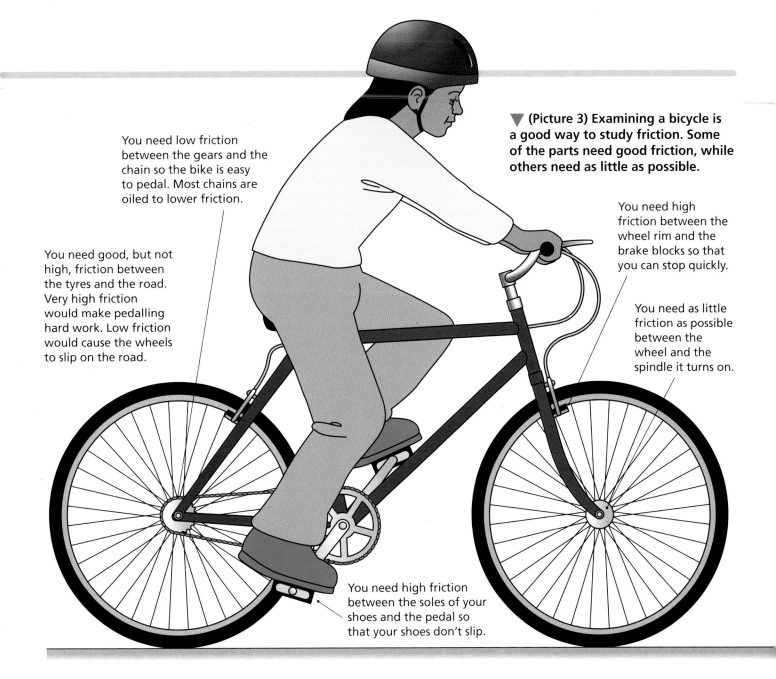

You need low friction between the gears and the chain so the bike is easy to pedal. Most chains are oiled to lower friction.

You need good, but not high, friction between the tyres and the road. Very high friction would make pedalling hard work. Low friction would cause the wheels to slip on the road.

▼ (Picture 3) Examining a bicycle is a good way to study friction. Some of the parts need good friction, while others need as little as possible.

You need high friction between the wheel rim and the brake blocks so that you can stop quickly.

You need as little friction as possible between the wheel and the spindle it turns on.

You need high friction between the soles of your shoes and the pedal so that your shoes don't slip.

You can get a better idea of what surfaces are like by looking at a sheet of sandpaper. This has easy-to-see bumps and troughs all over it. If you place one sheet of sandpaper on top of another and try to push one past the other you hear a gritty tearing sound. This is what it is like when any two objects rub against one another.

Can anything be frictionless?

Nothing in this world is frictionless. If it were, it would be impossible to handle because we could never get a grip on it. So friction is an important part of our world.

We need natural stickiness, but we also need to control it so that we can get a good grip when we want it, and less of a grip when we want things to move easily (Picture 3).

Summary
• Friction is natural grip.
• Friction is caused by rough surfaces.
• Nothing in our world is frictionless.

The rules of friction

The amount of friction changes with the force holding two objects together, but not with the amount of area in contact.

When we think about friction, we think about stickiness, or grip. So what does the amount of grip depend on? Here are two simple experiments that help you to decide the rules (laws) of friction. To do the experiments you need to be able to make a fair test.

Measuring force

To move a wooden block across a table, it must be pushed or pulled. This push or pull is called a **FORCE**.

The force needed to move the block has to be enough to overcome the grip between the surfaces. This is because friction is also a force, but one that works against movement.

Force can be measured by an instrument called a **FORCEMETER** (Picture 1).

Force is measured in a unit called **NEWTONS**. The unit is named after the famous English mathematician, Sir Isaac Newton.

Friction and area

Using a forcemeter you can find out if friction increases as more of the block is touching the table (Picture 2).

▼ **(Picture 1) You can use a forcemeter to find out how much friction there is between the block and the table.**

You can test a range of objects with a forcemeter.

Forcemeter

Table or other surface

The forcemeter tells you how much pull or push (force) is needed to overcome friction. Watch the scale as you try to pull the block. The scale shows the force you are using. The block will only move when you pull with more force than the friction.

Weblink: www.CurriculumVisions.com

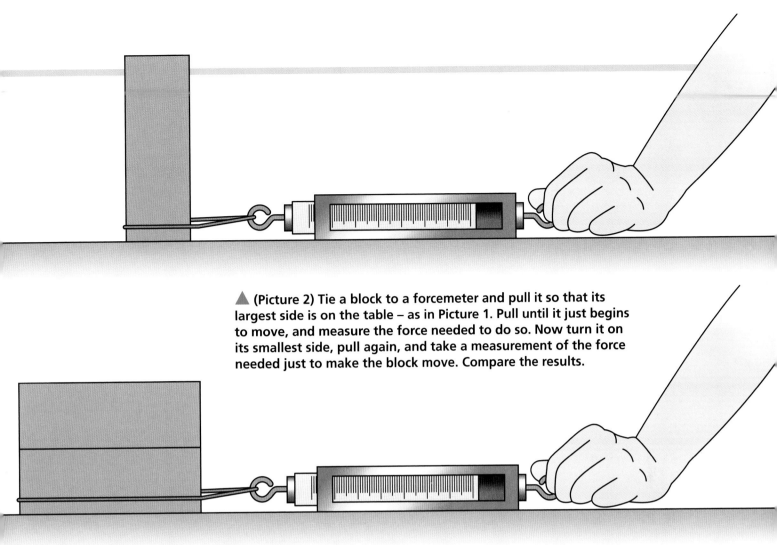

▲ (Picture 2) Tie a block to a forcemeter and pull it so that its largest side is on the table – as in Picture 1. Pull until it just begins to move, and measure the force needed to do so. Now turn it on its smallest side, pull again, and take a measurement of the force needed just to make the block move. Compare the results.

▲ (Picture 3) You can use a forcemeter to find out if the force is different when more blocks are added.

You should find that the force needed is the same in both cases. The amount of friction does not depend on how much of the block touches the table. If this result seems surprising, test it again.

Force on the surface

Try a second test to see what happens when you press, or force, the block down harder on the table. To do this, pile two blocks on top of one another and pull the bottom block with the forcemeter (Picture 3). You should find that the force needed to begin to move both blocks is twice as great as that needed to pull one block.

Add one more block and try again. You should find that the force needed to begin to pull this pile is now three times as great as that needed to pull one block.

From this we can tell that friction becomes greater as greater force presses the surfaces together.

Summary
- Friction is a force that pushes or pulls against movement.
- Friction does not depend on the amount of area in contact.
- Friction varies with the weight pressing one surface down on the other.

Weblink: www.CurriculumVisions.com

Which materials grip best?

Different materials grip each other by different amounts. This is what makes some materials more slippery than others.

You can **SLIDE** your hand over the top of a desk much more easily than over a rubber mat. If you are pressing down by the same amount each time, the stickiness (friction) between objects changes with each material you slide your hand over.
A mouse on a mouse mat is another example of something that slides (Picture 1). Rough and soft, **FLEXIBLE** materials grip best.

◀▼ (Picture 1) You may think the ball is what causes a mouse to slide, but it actually slides over the mouse mat on glides of plastic.

Testing materials

To test which materials grip well, you need something heavy, such as a brick, and a piece of carpet, a piece of vinyl flooring, a piece of rubber, a rubber band or sticky tape, and a forcemeter (Picture 2). Cut out a piece of carpet, wrap it around the underside of the brick and hold it in place with the rubber band or tape. Now pull the brick using a forcemeter and read the force needed just to get it to move. Repeat this test replacing the carpet with vinyl, and then rubber.

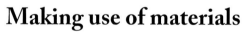

Glide

Glide

Making use of materials

If we know which materials grip best and which grip least, we can plan to use them where they will be most useful. For example, sticky rubber might be better than slippery plastic for a floor tile. You are less likely to slip and fall over on a surface with more grip.

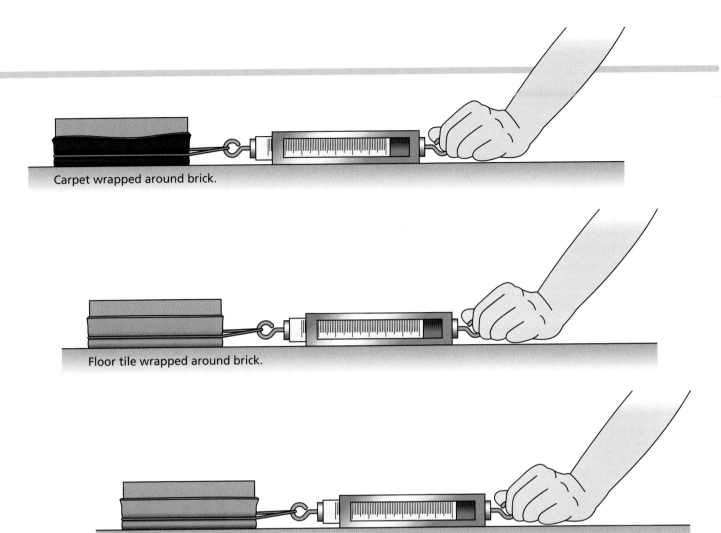

Carpet wrapped around brick.

Floor tile wrapped around brick.

Rubber wrapped around brick.

▲ **(Picture 2)** You can test the friction of various materials by wrapping them around a brick. Always drag the materials over the same surface and at the same speed.

▼ **(Picture 3)** You can control the way a kicked ball leaves the shoe by changing the materials used to make the shoe and the ball. Some materials have less friction between them.

Using different materials can have big effects in other ways, too. For example, by changing the materials of the ball and the shoe, the way a ball is controlled when kicked can be changed (Picture 3). This will affect how a game is played.

Summary

- **The amount of friction depends on how rough or flexible the material is.**
- **Materials with the smoothest surfaces have the least grip.**
- **Materials with the roughest surfaces have the best grip.**

Weblink: www.CurriculumVisions.com

Where a good grip is needed

You can increase friction by using suitable materials and making surfaces rougher.

If you try holding soapy dishes, or a bar of wet soap, you will find that they are quite difficult to hold. The dishes and the soap appear far less slippery, however, when you are wearing washing up gloves (Picture 1). Why is this?

When soap is wet, the little troughs in the surface fill with water and become smoother, so the bumps in your fingers can't grip the soap as well. Soap film, or liquid soap, on a dish work the same way.

Why soft is useful

Rubber gloves are made of a very soft material that squashes down into the troughs of the soap even when it is wet, pushing the water out. As a result, it gets a better grip. Soft rubber soles are used on athletic shoes (Picture 2) in part for the same reason: the soles give a good grip. Goalkeepers also have soft rubber surfaces on their gloves.
All cars have soft rubber tyres.

▲ (Picture 1) Washing up gloves have a pattern on them to help improve grip.

▼▶ (Picture 2) Soft soles are best for a good grip on hard surfaces. Notice the gaps in the tread so that water can be squashed out of the way if the surfaces are wet.

A good grip in the wet

Gripping surfaces have patterns cut into them. This is called a **TREAD**.

A tread is used because grip is very different when a surface is wet from when it is dry. When the weather is wet, a flat shoe sole or tyre can easily trap water between itself and the road. This will

(Picture 3) The tread on tyres provides a place for water to go when the tyres run over a wet road.

These zig-zag channels make up the tread and allow the water to be pushed out of the way, giving the tread a good grip on wet roads.

If the depth of the tread gets too shallow, the tyre is nearly worn out and there is an increased chance of AQUAPLANING.

cause the shoe or tyre to lose its grip. The tread (Picture 3) makes it easy for water to be squashed out of the way and keeps good grip even in wet weather.

Grip on ice and mud

When one of the surfaces is very slippery, you can get a better grip by making the other surface bite into the slippery one.

In many outdoor sports, for example, players use studded shoes. The studs dig into the soft, slippery ground and give extra grip for running faster.

Snowy and icy weather make roads very slippery. This can be especially dangerous for cars. In this weather, chains may have to be wrapped around tyres (Picture 4). The steel of the chain is harder than the ice so it bites into the ice and gives some grip.

▼ **(Picture 4)** If a hard material is to have a good grip, it must bite into the slippery surface.

Summary

- For a good grip, both surfaces need to be rough.
- Soft materials can squash down into surfaces to give a better grip.
- Hard materials can bite into slippery surfaces to give a better grip.

11

Getting moving

The friction between surfaces on the move is less than the friction when they are still.

Have you ever noticed that it takes less effort to keep something going than to get it moving in the first place?

Why friction changes

To get something to move you have to lift the tiny bumps of one surface out of the tiny troughs of the other. Once this has happened, as long as the object keeps moving, the bumps will not have time to settle back into the troughs and so the friction will be lower.

Fair test

You can prove that the force needed to keep something moving is smaller than the force needed to get it moving by using a forcemeter (Picture 1). You need to find the largest amount of pulling force just before the block starts to move, and the amount of force that will keep it moving.

▼ **(Picture 1)** Pull gently on a forcemeter until the block just begins to move. Have a helper read the scale and record the highest value they observed. Now pull the block along, and while it is moving, get your helper to read the scale on the forcemeter. It should be a smaller number.

Just starting to move

Moving

(Picture 2) An avalanche is a terrifying example of how much less friction there is when material is moving compared to when it is still.

The importance of moving friction

There are many places where the differences in moving and still friction are important. Here are just two examples to get you thinking.

Since starting a car moving needs more force than keeping it going, more stops and starts use more fuel.

Snow is held on steep slopes by friction. But if some of the snow is disturbed and begins to move (for example, if a skier jumps on it) the friction is reduced and the snow will continue to move. This can lead to a huge movement of snow called an **AVALANCHE** (Pictures 2 and 3).

Summary
- The amount of friction that builds up before an object moves is much higher than the friction needed to keep the object moving.

▼ (Picture 3) How an avalanche starts and develops. Once an area of snow starts moving, the friction is much lower, so the snow begins to speed up as it slides, gathering enough energy to cause damage.

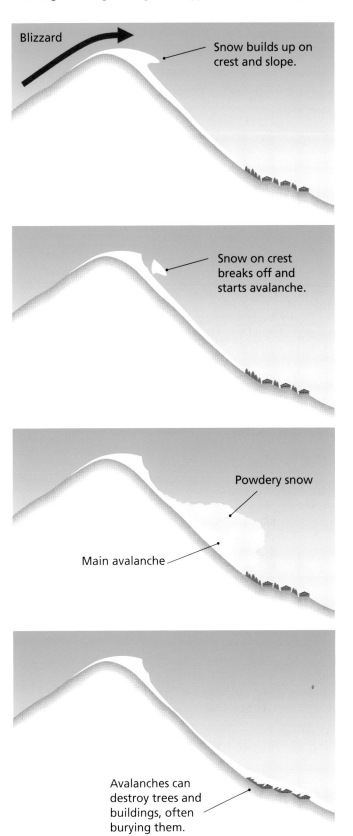

Blizzard

Snow builds up on crest and slope.

Snow on crest breaks off and starts avalanche.

Powdery snow

Main avalanche

Avalanches can destroy trees and buildings, often burying them.

Weblink: www.CurriculumVisions.com

Reducing friction

Friction can be lowered by adding liquids between surfaces. These liquids are called lubricants.

Have you ever tried to turn a door handle and found it stiff and difficult to move? This is because there is a lot of friction between the working parts. You can make the handle turn smoothly again by putting oil onto the moving parts.

A substance that is used to make one surface slip more smoothly over another is called a **LUBRICANT** (Pictures 1 and 2).

What lubrication does

When you put a liquid, like oil, between two surfaces, the oil spreads and clings to the two surfaces in a thin layer. Some of it may also fill in the troughs in the surfaces, making it harder for the bumps on one surface to sink down into the troughs of the other.

Oil is a liquid, and its particles can easily slide over one another. This means that the friction in the oil is small.

When you use oil you are actually keeping surfaces apart and letting layers of oil glide over one another instead.

▼ **(Picture 1) Oil is used to reduce friction on a bicycle chain.**

▶ **(Picture 2) How oil reduces friction.**

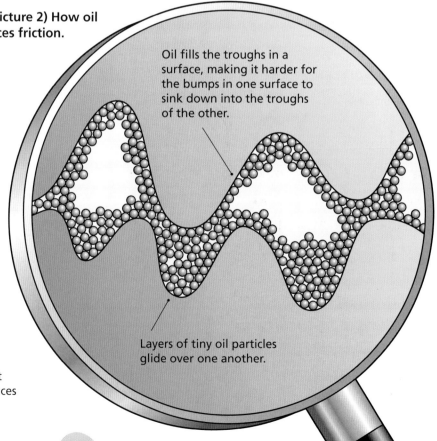

Oil fills the troughs in a surface, making it harder for the bumps in one surface to sink down into the troughs of the other.

Oil clings to most surfaces, so it does not fall off when the surfaces are upside down.

Layers of tiny oil particles glide over one another.

Weblink: www.CurriculumVisions.com

Testing lubricants

You can compare how well oil and other liquids, such as water, make things easier to move. First, measure the friction between two dry surfaces. Now make the surfaces wet and measure the friction again. Lastly, dry the surfaces and then oil them. Measure the friction a final time (Picture 3).

What makes a good lubricant?

Liquids stick to most surfaces, and so do not fall off. This is important if you want to lubricate something that is not level, such as a door hinge.

Oil is used to reduce friction instead of water, or some other liquids, because oil has many advantages. Oil is thin, meaning it flows easily, allowing one layer of oil to glide over another. A thicker substance, like syrup, would be stickier and make gliding much more difficult. Water also sticks to itself more than oil does.

Secondly, the liquid must not disappear quickly. Petrol, for example, **EVAPORATES** very quickly. Water also evaporates quickly. Oil, on the other hand, evaporates very slowly and stays on surfaces for a long time.

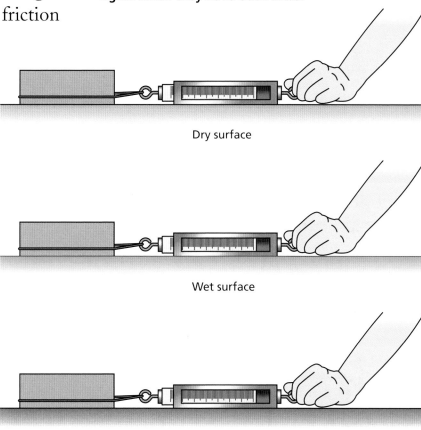

▼ (Picture 3) Test the effect of lubricants by using a forcemeter to measure the force needed to drag a brick when the surfaces are dry, when they are wet, and again when they have been oiled.

Dry surface

Wet surface

Oiled surface

Water makes a bad lubricant for another reason. If it is left in contact with metals for weeks and months, it combines with them. One example of this is the rough surface coat called rust.

Summary
- A liquid that allows two surfaces to slip more easily is called a lubricant.
- Oil makes a good lubricant because it is thin, clings to surfaces and doesn't evaporate.

Weblink: www.CurriculumVisions.com

Where slipperiness occurs

You can reduce friction by making one or both surfaces very smooth. This can be good or bad.

Although we mainly want to keep a good grip between surfaces, there are some places where we want the surfaces to be as slippery as possible.

Slides

A playground slide is one place where we want to have slippery materials. This is why we use a sheet of mirror-shiny metal or plastic for the slide (Picture 1).

▲ (Picture 1) A playground slide is one place where slipperiness can be fun.

Glides

Glides are pieces of material with a very low friction. Look on the underside of a computer mouse (page 8) and you will see some small patches of slippery plastic glides.

Polishes and waxes

If you wax or polish something, you give it a shiny, sometimes even a mirror finish.

Waxes and polishes work in part by filling in the troughs in a surface.

A wax, or polish, is made of a soft material that flakes easily when it is rubbed. By flaking when a force is put on it, the wax allows surfaces to slip over one another. Candles are often rubbed across saw blades to make sawing easier. However, the wax soon wears off and the surface must be rewaxed.

Skiing

Skiers (Picture 2) try to keep the amount of friction between their skis and the snow low. They do this by waxing their skis. The wax (which today is mostly an artificial substance) cuts down friction on the bottom of the ski.

Skiing over a ski run makes the ice smoother and this also makes skiing faster.

▲ (Picture 3) Cars will slide on ice, not just because it is smooth, but because a film of water forms under each tyre.

Ice skating

Slipperiness is very useful for ice skaters. Skaters need to be able to glide over the ice. But no wax or polish is used here. Instead, surfaces are made more slippery by using water.

▼ (Picture 2) Skiing can be made faster by waxing the underside of the skis.

One special property of ice is that it melts when a high pressure is put onto it. An ice skate is a thin blade that takes all the **WEIGHT** of the skater and uses it to press down on a narrow line of ice. As a result, the ice melts and the skater slips over a film of water.

Dangerous roads

When people drive on icy roads, ice under the tyres melts and the tyres cannot get a proper grip. This is one reason why an icy road is so treacherous (Picture 3).

Summary
- Friction can be reduced by using a wax or polish.
- Friction on ice can be reduced by melting the surface of the ice.

Weblink: www.CurriculumVisions.com

Rolling friction

The amount of friction that occurs when something rolls over a surface is far smaller than when it slides.

Friction makes things difficult to move. So how do we reduce friction without using oil?

Wheels and rollers

Friction is highest when we drag one thing over the other. A sledge, for example, drags one rough surface over another. But wheels, or rollers, use less friction across the surface. Instead, they roll over it (Picture 1).

When you use rollers or wheels, you need less than a thousandth as much force to move an object than if you dragged it across the ground. If you compare the effort needed to pull a stone slab on a sledge, and to push it over rollers, you will quickly see how much easier it is to roll something (Picture 2).

Simple rollers

The simplest roller is just a log from a tree. People in ancient times probably moved many of the giant slabs of stone that built monuments such as Stonehenge in England, or the Pyramids in Egypt, using rollers (Picture 3).

◀ (Picture 1) To see the difference between sliding and rolling, first push a bike across the playground. Now pull on the brakes and try again. You should be convinced that it is much easier to roll than to slide.

Weblink: www.CurriculumVisions.com

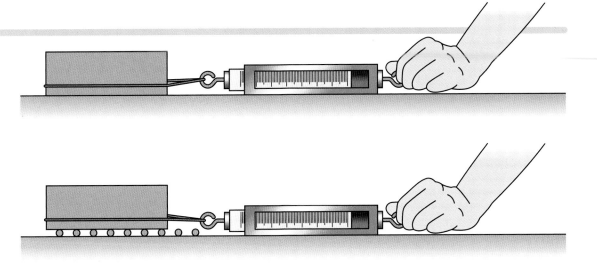

▶ (Picture 2) Use a forcemeter to compare rolling and sliding friction. First drag a brick along a table top and find the force needed to move it. Then put the brick on rollers and measure the force needed to move the brick.

▼▲ (Picture 3) Rollers are like wheels. Instead of sliding over a rough surface, they simply roll over. Rollers were probably used to move the giant blocks for Stonehenge, England, from their starting point in Wales.

Summary

- Rolling friction is up to a thousand times smaller than sliding friction.
- The discovery of the wheel changed the way in which people moved things.

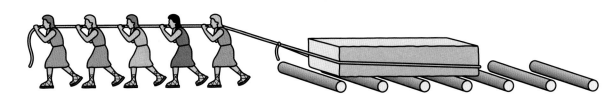

Weblink: www.CurriculumVisions.com

Water resistance

Friction in liquids, such as water, can be important. It can slow things down, but it can also speed them up.

Unless we move very fast on land, or in the air, we do not need to think about the way that air pushes against us as we move. However, water is a thick substance compared to air, so it is hard to move about in water even at slow speeds. The way that water pushes back on objects is called **WATER RESISTANCE**. It is friction in water.

The stickiness of liquids

Every liquid has its own unique stickiness. If you drop a marble in a jar of syrup, and at the same time drop another one in a jar of water, you will see the marble fall much faster in the water than in the syrup (Picture 1). The syrup is naturally thicker and more sticky than the water and so it is harder for the marble to move through it.

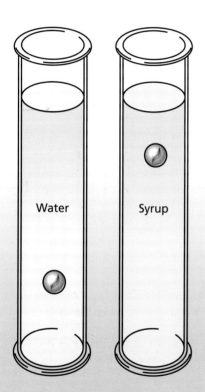

◀ (Picture 1) An object, such as a marble, will fall faster in water than in syrup because water is less sticky.

Water

Syrup

▶ (Picture 2) Viking longships cut through the water. They are an example of a streamlined shape.

Weblink: www.CurriculumVisions.com

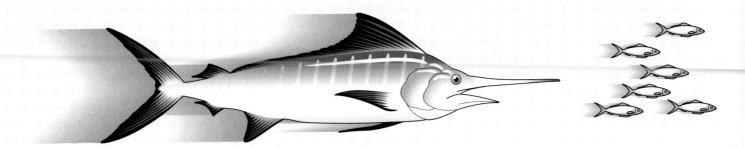

(Picture 3) Marlin are the supreme hunters of the open oceans. Despite weighing up to half a ton they have such a streamlined shape they can reach 60km/h and outpace the fish they are chasing.

You can see this in another simple test. Try moving a spoon about in a jar of water, then move the same spoon about in a jar of syrup.

Making boats move more easily

Boats are designed to move as easily as possible through water. One way to make a boat move more easily is to give the hull (the part in the water) a smooth surface.

Another way to make it easier for a boat to move through water is to give it a shape that 'cuts' through water easily. This is called STREAMLINING (Picture 2).

Natural streamlining

Fish and other water-living creatures have to be able to move quickly in water. The marlin can move through water at 60km an hour (Picture 3). Its body is streamlined, so it can cut through the water and allow the fish to move easily.

Fins, paddles and propellers

If we want to move on land, we push against the ground. When canoeists or motor boats want to move they have to push against the water. They do this using the opposite of streamlining. When canoeists move, they put the flat blade of the paddle into the water and push hard (Picture 4). Similarly, a fish pushes the flat of its tail and fins from side to side. As the tail and fins push against the water, the water pushes back and gives them the force they need for movement.

Summary
- **Water is a much thicker substance than air and so it is more difficult to move through.**
- **Boats and fish have to be streamlined to move easily through the water.**

(Picture 4) Canoeists push the flat blade of the paddle against the water to force themselves forwards.
  The canoe is also streamlined to cut through the water with as little resistance as possible.

Weblink: www.CurriculumVisions.com

Air resistance

Although the air seems thin, it is thick enough to slow down fast-moving objects.

When we walk about we do not usually notice the air. This is because air is naturally 'thin' and easily moves aside as we walk through it. However, when we move faster, the air does not move aside as quickly, and so we become aware of the air pushing back at us. This pushing is called **AIR RESISTANCE**.

If you hold a large sheet of cardboard in front of you and then run about, the friction of the air becomes very clear (Picture 1).

▼ **(Picture 1) If you run while holding a sheet of cardboard, you can feel the force of the air against the card.**

▲ **(Picture 2) Parachutes trap air as they fall. This slows their descent.**

Making use of air friction

The friction of the air can be very useful to slow something down, or to keep it in the air longer.

A parachute is an example of where the friction in air is used this way (Picture 2). The large parachute is designed to trap as much air as possible, allowing it to flow out of the sides slowly.

(Picture 3) Keeping down the air resistance on trucks means that they use less fuel and so can carry goods more cheaply.

Some seeds also use natural parachutes, or spinners. These are blades that catch the air as the seeds fall and slow down the rate of fall. In this way the seeds can be carried long distances by the wind before they fall to the ground.

Streamlining

Most often we want to keep the friction of the air very small. This means that we need to design things that cut through the air as easily as possible. Cars, trucks, trains and aircraft have streamlined shapes that cut through the air with as little resistance as possible (Picture 3). Birds also have streamlined shapes that help them fly easily through the air (Picture 4).

(Picture 4) Peregrines can dive at a staggering 440km/h. When they tuck their wings in they form a streamlined shape that easily cuts through the air. This helps them to catch other birds.

Summary
- Air resistance is only important if something moves quickly.
- Streamlining helps fast vehicles and birds move more easily through the air.

Weblink: www.CurriculumVisions.com

Index

Science@School

Teacher's Guide
There is a Teacher's Guide to accompany this book, available only from the publisher.

There's much more on-line including videos
You will find multimedia resources covering this and ALL 37 QCA Key Stage 1 and 2 science units as well as history, geography, religion and spelling subjects in the Professional Zone at:

www.CurriculumVisions.com

A CVP Book
Copyright © 2002–7 Earthscape

First reprint 2004. Second reprint 2006. Third reprint 2007.

Author
Brian Knapp, BSc, PhD

Educational Consultant
Peter Riley, BSc, C Biol, MI Biol, PGCE

Art Director
Duncan McCrae, BSc

Senior Designer
Adele Humphries, BA, PGCE

Editor
Lisa Magloff, MA

Illustrations
David Woodroffe

Designed and produced by
EARTHSCAPE

Printed in China by
WKT Co., Ltd

Volume 4E *Friction*
– Curriculum Visions Science@School
A CIP record for this book is available from the British Library.
Paperback ISBN 978 1 86214 140 7

Picture credits
All photographs are from the Earthscape Picture Library, except the following: (c=centre t=top b=bottom l=left r=right) Corbis 13tl.

This product is manufactured from sustainable managed forests. For every tree cut down at least one more is planted.